MW01290494

If you or yours tests, *Unwelcome* ~~...~~ *Greatest Challenges* is an essential read.

Richard Battle faced multiple tests in a short period of time and shares how he, with God's daily provision, overcame them.

You'll be glad you read his pilgrimage drawn from a period from when the world caved in on him!

Mike Huckabee, Former Governor of Arkansas, Two time U. S. presidential candidate, Author and commentator

As I began reading, Richard's story immediately captivated me, and I read his entire book in one sitting. Since we have been teammates on our senior softball team for several years, I thought that I was somewhat aware of Richard's challenges. However, page by page I soon began to understand the true magnitude of Richard's spiritual, emotional and physical journey. Two things really stood out for me: Richard's straight forward honesty and his deeply abiding Faith. To me Richard is a shining example of overcoming potentially devastating challenges through Faith. And I see his book as a divinely inspired guide for survival.

Joseph Dayoc III (Teammate and Fellow Cancer Survivor)

Unwelcome Opportunity is a masterfully written book that will have you counting your blessings more often. Richard Battle reveals much about himself through telling the powerful story about how he confronted major life challenges with faith, resolve, and reflection. It is a heartwarming story designed to inspire, not sadden the reader. No matter what you are experiencing in your own life, bad or good, you owe it to yourself and to your family to read and act on the very valuable life lessons this book imparts. Thanks, Richard, for passing along the wisdom of generations to all of us.

Dr. Robert Brescia
President & CEO, *STEM* Software,
LLC, Odessa, TX, and author of *Destination*
Greatness: Creating a New Americanism

"In my work as a Licensed Professional Counselor I am often called upon for comfort in times of grief. The loss of a marriage, the loss of health, the loss of a job, or the loss through death of a loved one, these are all times when people find themselves confused and lost. My first task as a counselor is to gently find where a grieving person places their hope. **Richard Battle has spent a lifetime planting and cultivating a profound source of hope in his Christian faith. In his book,**

Unwelcome Opportunity, he unpacks that hope for the reader, chapter by chapter, as he describes a terrible and frightening time in his personal life. Each chapter describes a specific stop on a harrowing journey through one of the most difficult years in a life that has had more than its share of difficult times. The loss of a marriage, changes in his career, and being forced to face the fragility of his body and his health, are not roadblocks but rather touchstones for Richard's deep and abiding strength and faith in scripture. Each challenge takes him further off his comfortable path but also takes him further and deeper on his faith walk, providing the reader with a model of hope to abide any troubles."

LuAnn Sandahl, Licensed Professional Counselor

ALSO BY
RICHARD V. BATTLE

Surviving Grief by God's Grace

*The Volunteer Handbook – How to Organize and Manage
A Successful Organization*

The Four Letter Word That Builds Character

The Master's Sales Secrets

UNWELCOME OPPORTUNITY

OVERCOMING
LIFE'S
GREATEST
CHALLENGES

RICHARD V. BATTLE

FOREWORD BY LARRY GATLIN

outskirts
press

Outskirts Press, Inc.
http://www.outskirtspress.com

ISBN: 978-1-9772-0164-5

Copyright Registration Number: TXu 2-100-055

All Scripture quotations, unless otherwise noted, are taken from *The Holy Bible, New International Version* from www.biblegateway.com

Cover photo © 2018 by Richard V. Battle and taken on April 14, 2018
Back Cover photo © 2018 by Richard V. Battle and taken on April 26, 2018

PRINTED IN THE UNITED STATES OF AMERICA

DEDICATION

To my dear friend Lolette May for the suggestion and on-going encouragement to document the story of my year of exceptional challenges.

To my good friend and long-time Spiritual mentor Dr. Logan Cummings who encouraged me to tell this story and who provided invaluable feedback during my endeavor to do so.

FOREWORD

Dear Folks,

When my old friend Ted McKnight asked me to read *Unwelcome Opportunity*, I told him I really didn't have time to read the book and really didn't want to but I would do it as a favor to him because he is my friend. A whole lot of folks want me to listen to their songs or read their books or give them advice in one way or another and while I try to be available to my fellow man, sometimes there are just too many of my fellow men and women to take care of. I hadn't finished reading the first page when I realized that I wasn't doing Ted a favor, but rather that my old friend, Ted McKnight, had done me a favor. This wonderful book was just what I needed at just the right time. Do YOURSELF a favor and read Richard Battle's new book, *Unwelcome Opportunity*.

Keep the Faith,
Larry Gatlin

Acknowledgments

There are so many people who contributed to this work by their treatment of my medical challenges, support of my needs and kindness extended to me.

I'm so grateful to my family for their support, assistance and commitment. Thank you to my brother Jerry and sister-in-law Cheryl Battle, my daughter Elizabeth and my family.

I would like to thank the doctors and medical staff for taking such good care of me

I appreciate the guys that shared pre-treatment times and the discussions we had.

I'm grateful to my teammates at Relentless Senior Softball for their support, and especially Joe Dayoc who shared some of the same challenges.

I appreciate the positive comments and encouragement from Jim McGee, Dr. Robert Brescia, Charles Larkam, Mike Huckabee, Kent Greene, LuAnn Sandahl, Alan and Cindy Goldsberry, Ted McKnight, Terry Boothe, Jud Wyatt and Scott Spears for this work.

Thank you to the team at Outskirts Press including Kirsten Ringer and Lisa Jones, for their assistance in bringing this project to life.

Thank you to Larry Gatlin for his kind words about this message in the Foreword.

TABLE OF CONTENTS

Introduction –
SPOILER ALERT!

Matthew 19:26 – "Jesus looked at them and said, '*With* man this is impossible, but *with God all things are possible.*'"

Life is funny. I had no desire to write about these experiences. My dear friend, Lolette May, who at the time was a development director for a major cancer organization suggested the idea in a conversation one day. She said that there weren't many books about men's experiences facing heart and/or cancer health issues, especially when such occurs in less than a year. She added that this story might inspire others facing similar challenges.

My former pastor and good friend, Dr. Logan Cummings, reinforced the benefit of sharing my experience when I disclosed it to him. His ongoing encouragement was priceless.

Once I accepted the idea, I thought that I would complete two business books in addition to the one that was already at the publisher and then work on this volume.

The Lord through The Holy Spirit working in me and through my two friends had another thought, and put onto my heart to complete this project with haste. I hope His purpose is that I may serve others sooner, and not because the time I have left to compose this story is limited.

I had an uncle who called me knothead when I was a kid whenever I got into mischief, which was too often. I'm sure that God has had justification for calling me that also for failing and disappointing him so many times. In spite of that, God's grace has been and is always bigger than my need.

Yes, I did have a pity party for myself, and am grateful that my long-time friend, Scott Spears, straightened me out. He reminded me that we all have challenges and trials and no one wants to hear someone feel sorry for himself. The experience reinforced the fact that when we focus on ourselves, we have a human tendency to see what we don't have instead of appreciating what we do have. When we focus on others, it is much easier to forget any troubles that we might be experiencing at the moment.

It is extremely humbling to proffer a volume about surviving a divorce after a long marriage, two heart stent procedures and a cancer diagnosis—all within ten months. I would rather not have had these experiences. Obviously, I'd rather have remained ignorant and outside of the club of others who have also experienced trials.

I am not a Biblical scholar. I'm not free from falling short of God's hopes or expectations from me. My objective within these pages is to share the Unwelcome Opportunity that I was presented and the Lord's blessings of renewed health, spiritual growth and the occasion to serve His plan.

Through my efforts alone, surviving the experience and documenting it for you would not have been possible. But with God's provision, I humbly submit it to you with the sincerest hope that you will find benefit from it.

My status while you are reading about my experience is in the Lord's hands.

THE SUMMIT

Jeremiah 29:11 – "For I know the plans I have for you," declares the Lord, "plans to prosper you and not to harm you, plans to give you hope and a future."

In September of 2016, I turned 65 years old. I felt as good and healthy as ever both physically and mentally.

The past three years had been tough at times. In spite of the prospects for the end of my long-term marriage, the future looked bright. My spirit was healing.

My faith had helped me to endure, knowing that the LORD would take better care of me than I deserved. I was comforted and given hope by the Scripture in **Jeremiah 29:11**.

I was grateful that I was healthy enough to play competitive tournament softball, which I'd resumed in 2010. After a fun season, I prepared to travel to Las Vegas for the annual World Masters Senior Softball tournament.

Within five days, I played in thirteen games and logged fifty-one miles of walking and running on my Fitbit. It was great fun, and best of all, I felt fantastic afterward.

My dream was to be able to play in the same tournament when I turned eighty-five, which was the oldest age bracket available. It gave me motivation to stay in great shape and focus on a long-range goal.

At that time, I didn't see any reason why I couldn't accomplish that goal.

I should have known that the future looked too good, and that more life lessons were on the horizon.

RICHARD V. BATTLE

THE PRECURSOR

Psalm 51:10-12 – "Create in me a pure heart, O God, and renew a steadfast spirit within me. Do not cast me from your presence or take your Holy Spirit from me. Restore to me the joy of your salvation and grant me a willing spirit, to sustain me."

When I arrived at the doctor's office for my annual physical in October of 2016, I felt great. During the examination, I was excited to share with the doctor my belief that I was more fit than most people my age. When I was younger, there were others who were always fitter than I.

Even though the doctor showed a little concern about the rise in my PSA, I was unconcerned. I thought PSA numbers had to be high to cause alarm. I learned later that the specific number didn't matter as much as a rise in the number over time.

The doctor suggested that I visit an urologist. I viewed it as an inconvenience. There was no way that I thought anything could be wrong because I felt so healthy. Besides, my mind was distracted with the pending change in my personal life.

The urologist thought that my PSA might be elevated for a reason that could be treatable by medication. He gave me a prescription and wanted another blood test after a couple of months. We both hoped that the PSA would drop. Again, I believed that this was a waste of time because of my good health. Little did I know at that time what was around the corner.

After a three-year separation, my long marriage concluded on Halloween. Not knowing God's full plan for my life, I felt like I had failed Him again.

I have always admired King David, who in spite of his failings, was counted as, "a man after God's own heart" in **Acts 13:22**. David's prayer of penitence in **Psalm 51** inspires me because of its contrition, sincerity and humility.

God's forgiveness of David's sins and failures encouraged me that I was still loved by God and could be used in His service. He has never failed or given up on me in spite of my many failures to glorify Him.

It was time to begin a new chapter in my life.

THE FIRST DENT
IN
THE ARMOR

Romans 8:28 – "And we know that in all *things* God works for the *good* of those who love him, who have been called according *to* his purpose."

THE STORM APPEARS

Matthew 8:24-26 – "Suddenly a furious storm came up on the lake, so that the waves swept over the boat. But Jesus was sleeping. The disciples went and woke him, saying, 'Lord, save us! We're going to drown!' He replied, 'You of little faith, why are you so afraid?' Then he got up and rebuked the winds and the waves, and it was completely calm."

I began November of 2016 with the sense of adventure. I was healthier than ever and had just concluded a long period of uncertainty.

There were a dwindling number of logistical issues that, once resolved, would enable me to focus on the future. While it wasn't my idea to embark on this new journey, I looked forward to the possibilities over the horizon.

On a gorgeous fall Saturday, my brother, Jerry, helped me to move some items into a storage building until I could determine the path ahead. It was a hard day with a lot of work, and I was grateful to have his help.

The next day, I started my daily four-mile walk eagerly. After about a quarter of a mile, I felt tightness in my upper chest. This was a new experience for me, and I didn't know what it meant. I didn't even consider that I might have a heart issue because of the great condition that I was in.

I decided to "walk it off" as I had been encouraged to do in every athletic endeavor that I had experienced. After about half a mile, the pain subsided and I shrugged it off as unimportant.

I began my next walk without thinking about the previous day's pain. Once again, after about a quarter mile, I felt the pain. This time, I wondered if it was worth consulting my doctor. Again, it subsided after about a half mile and I completed my walk.

The next day, I began my walk with a slight tinge of apprehension. When the pain returned after a quarter of a mile, I knew that getting it checked out was warranted. Since I was hard-headed, I again completed my walk.

After I returned home, I set up a doctor's appointment for the following Monday, and believed that I would be told it was nothing. If that happened, I would feel guilty for going to the doctor.

The rest of the week, I repeated my walks and had the same experience every day. Each day that I completed the walk, I wondered if I should cancel my doctor's appointment because I was imagining a problem.

On Saturday before my appointment, the pain showed up at the same time, but was significantly more intense than the previous days. This grabbed my attention!

Instead of resuming and completing my walk as during the previous six days, I quickly concluded that it was in my best interest to return home. I proceeded methodically and wondered if I would make it or not. Now I was very concerned and glad that I had not cancelled Monday's doctor appointment.

When I returned home, I rested, not wanting to risk the return of the sharp pain that I had just experienced. It was difficult not resuming my daily walk habit on

Sunday, but I decided to take it easy until the doctor discovered what was happening to me.

When I arrived at the doctor's office on Monday, my family physician wasn't in the office. His nurse practitioner entered the examining room to hear why I was there. I still had the hope that in spite of my pain, it would still be determined that a doctor visit was unnecessary.

As I recounted my experience to her she interjected "Stop" before I concluded. I asked her if she wanted me to stop telling her my story. "No," she said, "stop exercising!"

She recommended that I see a cardiologist as soon as possible. Instead of calling his office, she called him on his cell phone and emphatically requested that I be seen the next day.

Tuesday I went to the doctor's office to have my heart checked. When I entered the office, I looked healthier than the other patients in the waiting room, which further worried me about spending time with the doctor without a real reason. He calmly examined me and instructed me to return the next morning for a stress test and do not exert myself. Again, I worried about creating much ado about nothing.

The day before Thanksgiving, I arrived, hoping to determine that whatever I was experiencing was minor and that it wouldn't inconvenience me on Thanksgiving or for the football game on Friday.

My daily prayers included asking for good health for myself. After the pain had appeared, I more seriously requested the Lord's provision of good health. I had experienced enough ups and downs in life to know that God has and does take better care of me than I deserve every day.

Philippians 4: 6-7 is a Scripture that I think of when times are tough, as it provides me great comfort. – It instructs us, "Do not be anxious about anything, but in every situation, by prayer and petition, with thanksgiving, present your requests to God. And the peace of God, which transcends all understanding, will guard your hearts and your minds in Christ Jesus."

Several tests were administered to me that day. Even though I was still working, I did not worry about work. I felt a peace and didn't worry about how long I would be away from the office.

Images were taken in a process that did not reveal if there was any cause for alarm. The nurses commented on my excellent condition, and that I didn't look like a person with heart disease. That news made me feel good and contributed to my worry about wasting everyone's time.

I was wired up for the stress test, and again thought I would pass it with flying colors. As we began, it was easy. The nurse increased the incline and I still felt great. Then things took a turn and I began to wonder what was coming next.

Just before the nurse was going to pronounce me fit and without concern, I started to labor. She got a concerned look on her face, but remained calm otherwise. She abruptly stopped the test and disconnected me from the wires. The tests were now concluded, and now it was time to wait for the results from the doctor.

He entered the examining room without revealing anything in his expression. I would never want to play poker with my doctor because of the lack of emotion he displayed that day. I hoped for good news and a resumption of normal life.

Then he began with the news that would change my future. He showed me pictures from the imaging that revealed that my LAD (Lower anterior descending) artery, otherwise known as the "widow maker" was 80-90 per cent blocked. This was not something that could be healed with two aspirins and rest.

There was an additional blockage, but he spoke of it without cause for concern. After the news of the first blockage, any additional issues alarmed me more than they would have previously.

My concern about wasting doctor's time was not only unfounded, but almost kept me from obtaining the help I would need to save my life and go forward. I hope you will not hesitate if you feel unusual, but will have your health checked.

Having known that I was a high energy person with a stressful job, he prescribed specific steps. He braced himself for resistance from me, and was surprised when I agreed to his recommendation.

Immediately, he had me escorted to the hospital across a small street to be admitted. Everything had happened so quickly that I did not have time to fully understand what was going to happen next and the change it would cause in my life.

The storm which would change my future had arrived!

I'm Really Out of Control

Proverbs 20:24 – "A person's steps are directed by the LORD. How then can anyone understand their own way?"

One minute I was sitting in the doctor's office and the next I was in the hospital after a short stroll. It was probably better that way so that I wouldn't have second thoughts about what was about to happen to me.

The young lady escorted me into the emergency room, and several staff members scurried in to begin preparing me for what they called the "Cath lab."

I didn't exactly know what that meant then, and I will spare you as much technical jargon as possible. That also benefits me because it minimizes the chances that I will make a mistake. What happened is more important than the technical description.

I was questioned, prodded, poked and had to take my clothes off to put on the flimsiest of covers. If I didn't watch it, I could be arrested for flashing. Then, I was laid out and wheeled into the lab, which was well lighted and extremely cold.

Further preparations were made, and I was transferred to a table so thin that I worried about rolling off of and onto the floor. My right arm was tied onto an extension from the table.

Like most people, I like being in control of my life. In business and volunteer endeavors, I have been blessed to be charged with large responsibilities. Those opportunities can lead one to attempt to exercise more control over events. Experience demonstrates how impractical that is.

After losing my son, John, I had learned that I'm not in control of much, if anything. Thankfully, God is always in control. Whenever I begin feeling frustrated about not controlling a situation, I'm reminded of **Proverbs 3:5**, "Trust in the Lord with all *your* heart and *lean not on your* own understanding." It helps me to relax.

Finally, the doctor strode into the lab. He looked calm and confident, which made me feel better. He explained that they would give me an anesthesia that would not put me totally under, but would disable me from feeling or moving. He explained that they would make a small incision in my wrist and use it to transverse my artery into my heart. That is as technical as I can explain it.

I naively asked him if I could listen to a radio program while the procedure was conducted. He said that I could, but probably laughed under his breath at the request.

They injected me with the anesthetic, and I remember looking up at the ceiling. I said a last prayer to the Lord for his protection and help. Time seemed to stand still.

The next thing I noticed was the noise of the staff cleaning up the lab and preparing to take me to a room in the cardiac ICU area of the hospital. I didn't know how much time had passed, whether the procedure had been successful, or what was next, but I had survived it. I thanked the Lord.

From the time I entered the doctor's office that morning until the procedure was completed was only about three hours. This event that began a major change in my life occurred in less time than it took to watch a football game.

In addition, I had no memory of the radio program that played into my ears while everything transpired. Whatever knocked me out worked extremely well.

The doctor appeared and told me that everything went well. He said that another artery was about 40% blocked, but wasn't treated at this time. I would only have to spend one night in the hospital, and should be able to go home on Thanksgiving day.

If I had tried to control that day, I couldn't have.

If I had worried about the procedure, it wouldn't have helped one bit.

One advantage of being older with more life experiences is that my faith had grown to trust that God would take care of me that day and every day better than I deserved.

THANKSGIVING 2016

Psalm 100: 4 – "Enter his gates with **thanksgiving** and his courts with praise; give thanks to him and praise his name."

Thanksgiving was always a special day for me. More than twenty times, I had attended the annual football grudge match between Texas A&M and my Texas Longhorns. In other words, I was thankful for something that in the big picture wasn't very important. It wasn't the first or only time I was distracted from the important things in life.

Thanksgiving 2016 was different. I was very thankful to have survived the previous day, and increasingly became aware of how easily the results might have been different.

They call the widow-maker artery that name for a reason. Often, people's first notice of it is when they drop dead. I was fortunate and blessed because a number of events occurred through no merit of my own that enabled me to receive a life-saving treatment. Praise the Lord!

I felt good that morning because of my expectation of getting out of the hospital. Sleep was evasive the night before in spite of the medicines coursing my arteries. Light and noise outside of my room was non-stop. It felt like the staff was having a party. They say don't go to a hospital to rest, and now I knew what they meant.

I will elaborate more fully in the next chapter how my life would change following this event, but the first notice of this was when I ordered breakfast. The procedure was easy. Pick up the phone, dial the kitchen and order room service.

When I called to order breakfast, I discovered quickly that my diet would be different. I was only allowed to order a heart healthy meal. No bacon for me and egg whites only (I loved the yoke of an egg). Thank goodness, I could still have coffee!

Like the watched pot, I waited for the doctor to arrive to discharge me. He examined me, and gave me the good news that I would be discharged around 9:00 a.m. I was ecstatic and didn't focus as much as I should have on the remainder of his visit. He provided me information about diet, encouraged me to continue my exercise regimen and discussed follow-up visits. All I could focus on was getting out of the hospital!

After the doctor left, I jumped up, put on my clothes and waited. And waited, and waited, and waited. I wasn't able to leave the hospital until what seemed like an eternity after noon.

Needless to say, I was now more apprehensive about whether any little thing might cause me a bigger problem than I'd ever known before.

I was very grateful to have had family support so that I wouldn't be alone that day and night. All-in-all, this was my best Thanksgiving ever!

THE DAY AFTER
THANKSGIVING

Isaiah 41:10 – "So do not fear, for I am with you; do not be dismayed, for I am your God. I will strengthen you and help you; I will uphold you with my righteous right hand."

The day after Thanksgiving, I was grateful to be staying with family. I had gotten a good rest Thanksgiving evening and was appreciative to be in recovery mode instead of the other alternative.

In a departure from my normal activity, I did not jump up and begin accomplishing activities and tasks. I never seemed to be without something that needed to be done, and trying to clear my to-do list was a daily priority. Instead, I took things easy.

The shock of what I had experienced had not fully sunk in, and football games were a welcome diversion to keep me from trying to do too much, too quickly.

I had been spared death and would begin to contemplate why and what I was supposed to do with whatever additional time that I had on this earth.

Late in the day, I coaxed my daughter, Elizabeth, into taking a brief walk to begin my rehabilitation. She was welcome company and the pace was much more leisurely than my normal routine. **Isaiah 41:10** was the Scripture that she had included on her high school softball letter jacket. It was a tremendous reminder that I wasn't alone, or just with family, but that God was in control of my every breath.

Because of my new-found status, I thought it prudent to be taken back to my residence. In hindsight, it may have been premature, but it seemed right at the time. There I was all by myself.

While I rested better in my own bed than in the hospital, my consciousness was on guard for every breath and heartbeat. Was everything alright? Was my breathing ok? Was my heart rate ok? Did I need to see the doctor for any discomfort or pain that occurred? I was apprehensive because I didn't know what to expect regarding my breathing, heart-rate, discomfort or pain. If I didn't have faith that the Lord would take care of me regardless of what would happen, I would have gone crazy! I don't know how people without faith survive the adversities in life!

The next morning, I began a daily ritual of letting my brother, Jerry, and Elizabeth know that I was ok. I didn't want to pass away, and be undiscovered for several days.

Taking it easy and not returning to work or my regular exercise program too quickly was difficult for my type A personality. I was beginning to consider all of the changes that would help me going forward.

Changing My Daily Life

Proverbs 16:20 – "Whoever gives heed to instruction prospers, and blessed is the one who trusts in the LORD."

My natural tendency was to strain at the restraint on my normal activities and push to resume them as soon as possible. It is amazing how we humans can think that we're bulletproof in spite of life's experiences.

The day after I returned home, I began reviewing the stack of documents that I was given regarding the hospital stay and my insurance coverage.

The large stack of papers over-communicated to an extent that only an attorney might appreciate. I'm the kind of guy who likes information in a simple outline form. Then I can go down the list in order until completion.

As I highlighted the diet pages, I became discouraged. All of the foods that I liked were on the bad list: beef, Mexican food, chili, soups, cream gravy, milk fat, eggs, colas, hamburgers, fried chicken, ice cream and what seemed like an endless list of my favorites.

The good list had very little of anything that I liked except for water. Salads, greens and everything had to be low sodium. I loved salt.

Need I say that it wasn't, and is not easy.

While the instructions referred to in **Proverbs 16:20** refer primarily to heeding instruction from the Lord, I determined that if I had a chance of enjoying a long life of quality, I'd better change my ways.

Elizabeth told me that she wasn't through with me yet, and that she expected me to walk her down the aisle for her wedding in several years. Failing to live to give her away at her wedding would not only disappoint her, but is one of my biggest fears. Since I was 47 when she was born, I have known that I wouldn't see her achieve middle age. Now, I am facing a threat that might prevent me from seeing her married and beginning a family. These thoughts motivate me to live as healthily as I can in order to be there for her as long as possible.

I also want to savor retirement, travel, enjoy my friends and play softball when I am eighty-five at the World Masters Tournament in Las Vegas. I had plenty to live for that was far more important than any food or drink.

I had not spoken to the doctor about any limitations on exercise. While I didn't want to climb Mt. Everest, I hoped to resume golf, softball, fast walking, lifting weights, biking and anything that a normal 40-year-old could do. As you can see, I don't like accepting my age.

These questions and others were on my list for my first follow-up visit with the doctor. While I felt pretty good, I needed that expert affirmation that only a doctor could provide.

When I went into the cardiologist's office, again I felt like an Olympic athlete compared to others I saw awaiting their appointments. It showed me that our health is more than how we appear on the outside, and I may or may not have been in better health than any of them.

Thankfully, my doctor was pleased with my progress and said that everything was going well. I was relieved!

Now, it was time for an extremely important question regarding my quality of life.

"Will I be able to resume playing softball, and if so, in what period of time?" I asked. I waited for his answer, apprehensive of what I might hear.

He asked questions about how much running I would be doing. He told me that I should keep my heart rate below 130 beats per minute to minimize stress on my heart and the stent, and to reduce the risk of heart issues or stent failure.

Then he said the magic words, "You can resume playing softball..." He added, "But I would wait until eight weeks after the procedure."

I was ecstatic! Since it was December, I would be able to resume play at the beginning of the 2017 season. It was an important piece of resuming a normal life.

My daily prayers were more sincere than before my heart stent. I was grateful to be alive, and thankful for so many of the small things I experienced in life. While I fall short, I try to live out, **Ephesians 5:20** – "always giving thanks to God the Father for everything, in the name of our Lord Jesus Christ."

The First Interlude
Reflection and
Renewal

1 Corinthians 2:9-10 – "However, as it is written: 'What no eye has seen, what no ear has heard, and what no human mind has conceived'— the things God has prepared for those who love him—these are the things God has revealed to us by his Spirit."

Normal. All I wanted was to return to the normal life I had before I received the stent. When I hear people talking about a *new normal* for certain things, I now fully understand what they mean.

On the outside, everything appeared and felt normal, while on the inside there was a *new normal*. In me there was an active conflict between my feeling bulletproof and feeling that I had a ticking time bomb inside my chest waiting to explode.

I was grateful that my family and many friends were there for me. My pride wanted to save their caring and support for tougher challenges so I wouldn't wear them out. Those days would come sooner than I thought, and demonstrate that I shouldn't be such a hardhead.

While I began the search to learn the lessons I was supposed to learn from this experience, a previously-learned lesson helped me immensely.

After I lost my son, John, I shared the many lessons I learned in **Surviving Grief by God's Grace**. Later, I learned another one that helps me in difficult times. I hope it can help you.

People are inclined to ask, *Why Me?* when difficult times appear. I discovered that is not the correct question to ask as it only looks in the rearview mirror. We may or may not have done anything to cause our situation.

When difficulty arises, I believe the proper question to ask ourselves is, What *now*? This question looks into the future and is focused on learning the lesson or lessons that will help enable us to be more productive, serve others and glorify God. I find that when I focus on the future and what I'm supposed to learn, it is easier to experience a setback and move forward.

Graphically, these questions look like the simple chart below.

← Why me?   (Me)   What now?→
Looks backward   Looks forward

While none of us like to suffer or experience trials, they will inevitably happen. If they are going to happen, I pray fervently that I can learn the lesson or lessons that I am supposed to learn so that I don't have to suffer a second time to learn one lesson.

We also have the choice when adversity arrives to get closer to God for His grace, comfort and provision, or to drift further away from Him. In other words, you can attempt to solve your problem yourself, or you can lean on Him for His help.

J. Vernon McGee, of *Thru The Bible* renown, used a school paddling as an example. A friend told him that if he would back closer to the principal who was paddling him that the pain would be less than if he tried to move away from the principal, which is our normal reaction. McGee asserts, and I agree, that this is a similar principle as in our relationship with God. When trouble arises due to our weaknesses, we best serve ourselves when we get closer to Him.

December through February saw me return to as much normalcy as possible. I made new friends, resumed my exercise program, prepared for a new softball season, resumed my volunteer efforts, enjoyed announcing and attending Elizabeth's high school softball games and worked as much as before in spite of the doctor advising to de-stress my life.

The biggest change in my daily life was the major overhaul in my diet! Gone was beef, fried food, gravy, chili, hamburgers, French fries, hot dogs, bacon, eggs, ice cream, milk chocolate and as much salt as I could get rid of. I supplemented raw almonds, non-processed turkey, chicken and fish, added greens and substituted sorbets for ice cream. I wasn't perfect, but I strove to do the best I could in order to have the best quality of life for as long as possible. The good news was the change in diet led me to lose fifteen pounds.

THE SECOND DENT IN THE ARMOR

John 16-33 - "I have told you these things, so *that* in me you may have *peace*. In this world you will have trouble. But take heart! I have overcome the world."

THE STORM REAPPEARS

2 Corinthians 1:3-5 - "Praise be to the God and Father
of our Lord Jesus Christ, the Father of compassion and
the God of all comfort, who comforts us in all our troubles, so that we can comfort those in any trouble with
the comfort we ourselves have received from God. For
just as the sufferings of Christ flow over into our lives, so
also through Christ our comfort overflows."

When spring is fighting winter for dominance, you
have warm fronts fighting cold fronts. Occasionally,
you may have a warm front advance and retreat, and
then advance again. The resulting warm, cold and then

warm weather in a short period of time is abrupt, and makes people scratch their heads when they unexpectedly experience this type of change.

As I'm writing this outside of Austin, Texas we just experienced the phenomenon. One day our temperature was 84 and the next it was 41. The following day it was 70 again and rising.

I experienced a similar circumstance in March of 2017. I was feeling better and better and believed I was on the path to a full recovery from my heart stent.

Toward the end of the month, I began feeling discomfort. I wish I knew then what I know now, but isn't that true for all of us? The pain ebbed and flowed, which kept me from going to the doctor to have it checked out. Finally, on Friday the 24th, a friend persuaded me to go to the doctor.

Because of my experience in November and having an additional artery blocked around 40% at that time; my doctor had the staff prepare me to insert another stent into that area. It was supposed to be quick like the previous procedure. I had always wished that they fixed both of the arteries during the first procedure.

Just like before, I was rolled into the Cath lab and given the anesthesia. The similarity to my previous experience ended there.

I regained consciousness like before and the staff was completing their follow-up procedures, but I was informed that a stent had not been inserted as planned. Great, I thought. What now?

The doctor appeared and informed me that the location of the blockage was at an intersection of two arteries. Because of its complexity, they wanted to have two doctors involved in the procedure in case complications occurred. This would require me to transfer to a Round Rock hospital as it could not be done in Lakeway. That couldn't be scheduled until Tuesday. When I was told that I couldn't leave the hospital, I began to regret waiting until Friday to go to the doctor. I would have to spend several days in the hospital before I could receive the needed stent.

There are many jokes that would fit my feelings about my restriction to the hospital for the weekend, but I was not in a laughing mood.

On Saturday, I was examined by more doctors, and it appeared that my pain was heartburn caused by spicy food. I had not wanted to give up my salsa and chips, but I had been advised to do so because of the blood thinner that I was taking.

After this discovery, I hoped to be released and resume my weekend. No such luck. The doctors wanted to proceed with the Tuesday procedure and keep me in the hospital all weekend. I'm not sure how much of their insistence was based on the advice of their lawyers and how much was based on my health.

Seeing that I could not win that argument, I pushed to move the procedure up to Monday. They said that they would see what could be done.

So there I was on Saturday and Sunday in a hospital room with restricted movement. It bored me out of my mind and I got very little sleep, which is all I will say about the experience as I may have to return to that hospital someday.

I was grateful to feel the comfort of God throughout this time. He was with me and provided me the strength I needed. There was no way for me to know what was coming or when, and again I was unable to control circumstances. I hope the sharing of my experiences can help comfort you in some way in whatever challenge you are facing.

The one good thing that happened was that they thought that the procedure could be moved up to Monday. I hoped and prayed that it would be so and waited.

RICHARD V. BATTLE

In the Palm of The Lord's Hand

Psalm 18: 2 – "The LORD is my rock, my fortress and my deliverer; my God is my rock, in whom I take refuge, my shield and the horn of my salvation, my stronghold."

After two boring days in the hospital, I was more than ready for something to happen. Once again, I had no control over what would occur next or when. Once again, I decided to relax and let God direct the day.

Soon after breakfast, I was told to get ready to transfer to Round Rock for the procedure. At the time, it meant holding the plastic disposal bag with my belongings in my hand and waiting.

Like a little kid waiting for Santa to appear, I waited and waited for the required ambulance transportation to Round Rock. They finally arrived and began to prepare me to leave. I felt better and sensed guilt about not walking to the ambulance or driving myself. They took my vital signs and executed the transfer paperwork with the hospital. Everyone had to protect themselves in case they broke the package, which was me.

I had never ridden in an ambulance before, and I had mixed feelings during the ride. It felt weird riding in that medical vehicle when I felt ok. I thought more than once about how much it cost for that transportation compared to almost any other alternative.

The best part of the ride was my discussion with the medical technician. He loved his job, but I discovered that he was writing a novel about first responders. The lines he read me from his manuscript were very interesting. Since I had three books published at that time, I discussed the publishing process and offered to share any ideas that would help him. Again, it was strange having that discussion in light of what was about to occur that day.

Upon arrival at the hospital in Round Rock, which I had never seen or known of, they wheeled me inside on a gurney. I felt good and looked healthy. As I observed people looking at me, I wondered what they were thinking. Again, it was a strange first experience. I should have been grateful that I was conscious and not being brought in injured from a car wreck or worse.

It was as if I had drawn a Monopoly card that entitled me to advance directly to go. There was no delay for paperwork or questions. Immediately, I was taken into pre-op.

I was to wait for a cardiologist whom I had never met or spoken to before. The nurse in pre-op told me that he was the head of the cardiac department at that large hospital group for a large area around Austin.

His expertise was critical to me because I was informed that they may not be able to go through my wrist again. If he couldn't accomplish that, my recovery would be longer at a minimum. In addition, the risks of the procedure would increase.

If the doctor could not utilize my wrist, he would have to go through my groin, or worse, my chest. You can imagine which alternative that I was hoping would happen.

As the nurse prepared me, and I waited for the doctor, I knew that circumstances were not under my control, but in God's hands. Since I couldn't do anything but wait, I relaxed. I started seeing everything through a humorous lens and began joking with the nurse. Considering what was about to happen to me, she probably thought that I was crazy. I love humor, and often see it during the toughest of times. It serves me to defuse tension.

Finally, the doctor I had been eagerly awaiting entered the room with the command of a field general. He was calm and confident, but he issued instructions to the nurse and requested the images to see what his challenge was and any specific information about me. I'm not easily impressed, but he earned my respect almost immediately.

After studying my records, he came to speak with me. He stated that he didn't know which method of entry would be required to successfully complete the procedure. He looked at my wrist and examined the small scab that remained after Friday's failed stent attempt. I waited with some apprehension, not because of any potential complexity, but hoping for a quick recovery as in the previous procedure.

He finally stated that he thought he could go through the wrist, but he wouldn't know for sure until he was in the middle of the procedure and dealing with my heart directly instead of through images.

They completed my preparations, and wheeled me into the cath lab, which was somewhat similar to the one I had been in before. They moved me from the gurney type bed on wheels that they brought me into the lab onto the narrowest table. Again, I was as concerned about falling off of that table as I was of anything else.

I thought of **Philippians 4: 6-7**, which says, "Do not be anxious about anything, but in every situation, by prayer and petition, with thanksgiving, present your requests to God. And the peace of God, which transcends all understanding, will guard your hearts and your minds in Christ Jesus."

I said a last prayer and turned everything over to God, not knowing if I would awake, or if I did what the results would be. I was now in the palm of God's hand, and totally dependent on His benevolence to me.

They injected me with the anesthetic, and I lost consciousness.

His Gift of Mercy

Psalm 4:1 – "Answer me when I call to you, my righteous God. Give me relief from my distress; have mercy on me and hear my prayer."

Psalm 28:6 – "**Praise** be to **the Lord**, for he has heard my cry for mercy."

The next thing I knew, I was being wheeled into a room in the cardiac ICU unit. Another doctor stopped me to explain what they found and the procedure that had been done. To be frank, I was still coming out of the anesthesia, and didn't retain much of what he said.

I did recognize that the Lord had granted me mercy and thanked Him for it.

I was thankful that my brother, Jerry, and sister-in-law, Cheryl, were there for me. Jerry recounted the doctor's presentation to me later after I regained my senses.

They had inserted a stent in my circumflex artery and a balloon in the artery that teed into it. What complicated everything was that the stent was required right at that tee. I was ecstatic because they were able to enter my wrist, which meant a speedier recovery and only one more night in the hospital.

I have not seen or spoken to the cardiologist that performed my second stent since that day, but I did submit a glowing review of his work on me. He reminds me of *The Lone Ranger*. He rode into town, took care of the problems and left without waiting for any recognition or rewards. I am ever grateful to him!

Jerry picked me up the next morning and took me to his house. While I felt well, I was definitely weak and appreciated the opportunity not to spend that first night alone. Cheryl prepared a great evening meal and Jerry and I listened to an internet audio broadcast of Elizabeth's high school softball game after dinner.

While I could have stayed with Jerry and Cheryl longer, I was mentally ready to get home the next day. I took everything slowly until Friday and then I had a day that challenged the limits of the Lord's mercy.

It began as a normal day, but ended with gratefulness that I didn't suffer for pushing myself too far. That morning, I travelled into Austin to have lunch with friends who were in the Jaycees with me in my earlier days. We get together several times a year, which gives us an excuse to remain connected.

I was unable to return home in time for a 1:00 p.m. product review meeting that I was going to call in to attend since my travel was restricted. It took me six months to get the owner of our company scheduled to participate in this meeting, and I had several topics that I wanted to discuss for our future business. My only option was to pull over to the side of a busy roadway. The noises around me were quite distracting. The call lasted three hours, and I felt stressed almost the entire time. While it was successful, I questioned during the entire time whether I should have participated.

Later that evening, I resumed my position as the public address announcer for Elizabeth's high school softball team. I loved being involved in the game, and watching her in her senior season. I couldn't imagine how anything I enjoyed so much could add stress to my day, but it did. By the end of the game, I was spent and ready to go home and rest.

I'm sure the Lord thought about His gift of mercy, and the lack of respect I showed Him by abusing myself so soon after the procedure. After that day, I took a more measured schedule resuming my activities. There is no percentage of success in continually testing God's grace and mercy.

The Second Interlude – Rinse and Repeat

Psalm 66:20 – "Praise be to God, who has not rejected my prayer or withheld his love from me!"

After that trying Friday, I resumed my new normal activities quickly. I went back to work, began my daily
exercise regimen, resumed playing softball, enjoyed
some country and western dancing and continued my
new heart healthy diet.

It was a reboot of my new life and future. On my follow up visit a week after the procedure, my doctor told me that I should have a normal remaining life span, and be able to resume all of the activities that I enjoyed. Basically, the doctor's instructions were to "rinse and repeat" the instructions he had given me the previous November.

The Lord had answered my prayers and granted me mercy. He always loves me more than I deserve!

I wondered if I missed the lesson or lessons that I was supposed to learn from my previous heart event. Worrying about that wasn't worth it, I decided, because it wouldn't make any difference.

We're admonished in **Psalm 55:22** which says**, "Cast your** cares on the Lord and he will sustain you; he will never let the righteous be shaken." It is so difficult to let control go to God because we want to retain it. When we turn the responsibility of outcomes over to Him, we can trust that He will take better care of us than we can take care of ourselves. That doesn't mean that we won't suffer here or die, but it does mean that He takes care of us with His eternal perspective.

Spring turned into summer and I continued to feel better and become more confident about my recovery and good health.

My PSA registered 4.2 during my fall 2016 physical, which alarmed my primary care physician. Following his recommendation, I saw a urologist, who prescribed antibiotics. His hope was that the high number was caused by an infection.

On my next test, my PSA registered 4.8. My urologist was concerned, but decided to delay further action because this test was so close to my last stent. I was so happy to be recovering from the stents that I was oblivious to the seriousness of the PSA reading.

Mid-summer, I had another blood test, and this time the PSA read 5.2. The urologist was almost insistent on action, and I consented to have an MRI test. This revealed that I had three spots that he wanted to examine further. He said that it was likely to be cancerous and of an aggressive variety. Again, I didn't take the news too seriously because I felt well.

Need I tell you that by this time I was extremely fatigued in dealing with doctors and hospitals? I had been blessed in life to have only spent one night in a hospital before my first stent and that was in 1964. I had also been blessed with good health and minimal need to see doctors for almost all of my life.

I relented to the next recommended test, which was a biopsy. Little did I know how its revelation would further change my life.

THE THIRD TIME
IS THE CHARM,
OR IS IT?

Hebrews 11:1 – "Now faith is confidence in what we hope for and assurance about what we do not see."

The Foretelling

Exodus 23:20 – "See, I am sending an angel ahead of you to guard you along the way and to bring you to the place I have prepared."

When I looked back after my son's passing, I could see instances in which God had prepared me to endure it and survive. The experience proved to me that God always prepares us for where He is taking us, and He protects us throughout our lives.

I continued to feel better and better, and enjoyed my normal life. Unlike stories that I had heard, I had no symptoms that are connected with cancer and therefore thought it was unlikely that any test would reveal it when everything was said and done.

My most serious concern as I experienced the biopsy was one of pride. The procedure was invasive enough that I had to let some of my pride go before it occurred. I would soon learn that I had more pride to let go of, but that day was all I was focused on at the moment.

In an hour or so, it was over. I left the doctor's office more focused on taking care of my business responsibilities than I was with my health.

Without worry or concern, the rest of the day of the test was exceptionally good. I cherished reconnecting with a friend, enjoyed my new truck and felt great.

I gave no thought to receiving the test results, which I expected in a day or two. I think part of God's preparation was to take any worry off of me because it would not have benefitted me in any way. I'm thankful to Him for that.

I awoke on August 10, 2017 and anticipated another terrific day like the previous one. However, that day would be unlike any other one in my life to that point.

The Ground Shakes

Romans 5:2-5 – "…through whom we have gained access by faith into this grace in which we now stand. And we boast in the hope of the glory of God. Not only so, but we also glory in our sufferings, because we know that suffering produces perseverance, perseverance character; and character, hope. And hope does not put us to shame, because God's love has been poured out into our hearts through the Holy Spirit, who has been given to us."

The book of Romans has always appealed to me, and chapter 5, verses 2-5 especially resonates with me. It is easy for me to "hope in the glory of God". What is difficult is taking a single sentence that transcends suffering to hope. It is easy to read, comprehend and desire those words to be true. What can be overwhelming without God's grace are the depth, breadth, width and number of experiences that it takes to traverse that sentence.

This day delivered one of those experiences that I hope moves me closer to boasting about the glory of God. In addition to a day full of business activity, I had to travel to the Texas DMV (department of motor vehicles) on August 10th to renew my driver's license. That is always about as much fun as a root canal. I thought the process might be quicker if I reserved an appointment time and traveled to another office further away that was less utilized.

Thankfully, I'm not superstitious. In fact, I always use a line when someone else says something about luck. "It's bad luck to be superstitious," I say to the disbelief and laughter of the individual making the statement.

When I arrived at the DMV, I discovered that the reservation I made on-line wasn't in their system. A representative blamed it on a new software program. Taking a number, I resigned myself to a couple of hours just to have my picture taken and hand over some of my hard-earned cash. I don't have to tell you that I was not a happy camper that afternoon.

While waiting and minding my own business, the phone rang. Normally, I would not have answered it, but I thought it could be about the test results. Another opportunity to exhibit superstition was about to occur.

The doctor that administered the biopsy asked to make sure it was me, and said that he had the test results. He was in a hurry and in a matter of what seemed like two seconds the bomb dropped.

"You have cancer in one of the biopsied areas. It is important that you know your Gleason score in speaking to the other doctors. It is a four plus four equals eight." When I heard the word cancer, I thought how ironic that I received the news while doing something that wasn't enjoyable.

I felt the ground shake, but something was different. In 1992, I was close enough to an earthquake to be awakened, see clothes swaying in the closet and observe other hotel guests opening their doors to see what was going on. It was a helpless feeling, but in that experience I didn't shake. I looked around and everything appeared normal. In this instance, I was shaking--not the ground.

I didn't comprehend much else of what he said because in spite of the foretelling, I was unprepared to hear the facts of the test. I was hoping that the results would be negative, and I could resume my daily life.

Hanging up the phone, I had a surreal feeling as my mind began racing, and all of the other people waiting to conduct their DMV business seemed in a different place. Although they had no idea of the news I just heard, I wondered if my expression or the look on my face exposed my shock.

While I continued to wait, it dawned on me that the test results meant that this was only the beginning of an unknown amount of time and procedures with doctors and medical staffs to address my newfound challenge. My mind began thinking of the impact of this news on my daughter, Elizabeth, other family and friends, my business responsibilities and other commitments that I had. It was a time to focus on important things and not worry about things that previously seemed important, but weren't in the larger scheme of things. Deciding on when and how to tell Elizabeth was the most important one in my thoughts.

After what seemed like an eternity, I was finally called to complete the brief picture and money transfer. Somehow, I was able to function without belying my true feelings and then headed home. The picture on my driver's license was taken just after receiving the sobering news that I had prostate cancer.

I knew better than to wish it were a dream because I had experienced that disappointment when my son, John, passed away. Now it was on to discovering what needed to be done to rid me of this disease and taking action.

Taking the Bull
by the Horns

Exodus 14:15-16 – "Then the LORD said to Moses, 'Why are you crying out to me? Tell the Israelites to **move on**. Raise your staff and stretch out your hand over the sea to divide the water so that the Israelites can go through the sea on dry ground'."

In the *Living Bible* **version of Exodus 14:15**, it says, "Then the Lord said to Moses, 'Quit praying and get the people moving! Forward, march!'"

By the time Israel reached the Red Sea, they had seen God's hand save them on the evening of Passover, and be freed from slavery in Egypt. In spite of this, when Pharaoh and his army pursued them, they were frightened. God wanted them to move in order for Him to gain glory through what He was going to do next. As you know, Israel marched on dry ground through the parted Red Sea and the Egyptians were drowned.

Too often we think if we stand and watch, God will take care of us. He wants us to move on by faith in Him that He is in control and will provide for our every need according to His plan for us.

Once I had processed the news of my cancer, I determined it was time to take the bull by the horns. For those of you not familiar with that phrase, according to Webb Garrison in *Why You Say It*, it arose as a description of steer wrestling in cow camps. We use it today to describe someone who takes a problem head-on and doesn't wait. I was proactive and determined to take care of my end of the fight to beat all of my health challenges.

I had an August 28th follow-up with my urologist, who was out of the country. In spite of prostate cancer growing slower than some other cancers, I did not want to wait to begin the treatment.

Because of my previous heart stents and being on blood thinners, it was recommended that I not have surgery for a year after the last stent. In fact, I had to go off of the blood thinner for five days to have the biopsy. I'm grateful that a clot didn't occur during that time because it could have been fatal, making the cancer a non-issue.

In addition, I perceived radiation may be as effective with fewer side effects so I was leaning that way. I was recommended a radiation oncologist and I set an appointment.

Based on my tests, he recommended forty-five radiation treatments, which would occur five days a week for nine weeks. The commitment to drive into town daily for nine weeks seemed daunting at the time. I asked him why forty-five instead of the five that I had seen advertised. His opinion was that the same radiation dose would be administered, and the side effects would be less if the dosage was spread over forty-five treatments instead of five. That made sense to me, and I accepted that treatment.

Next, came the tough part. Because of the aggressive nature of my tumor, he recommended a hormone treatment for eighteen months that would significantly remove testosterone, as it is believed to be food for the cancer. The likely side effects of this semi-annual regimen seemed worse than those of the radiation.

Additionally, he wanted a bone scan to see if the cancer had spread outside of the prostate. I hadn't even thought about that possibility, or the complications it could add to the road ahead. I was grateful that the Lord is in control, had an eternal plan for me, and whatever happened would further that plan unless I got in the way.

I had the bone scan, which took almost half a day out of my schedule by the time everything was completed. My thoughts jumped back and forth between taking care of my business and other responsibilities and wondering what news I would hear. During the test, I listened for any clues from the technician, but there were none.

My oncologist called me the next day and said he had good news. I was appreciative because there didn't seem to be much of that lately. The bone scan was negative, which means my cancer had not spread outside the prostate.

When I returned to my urologist's office on the 28th, he expected to provide me the diagnosis and discuss alternative treatment options. He was very surprised to learn that I had not waited for him, but had begun the process with his associate.

They gave me the first of three injections of Lupron that day. Its effects would reveal themselves over time.

Davy Crockett's admonition was to, "Be sure you're right and go ahead." I was committed to a treatment path and felt confident of my decision. I would continue to study my cancer. I soon discovered that everyone's case is unique and that there are many more combinations of options than I'd considered. Again, I trusted myself in the palm of the Lord's hand.

THE THIRD INTERLUDE –
THE PHONEY WAR

Isaiah 40:31 – "But those who hope in the LORD will renew their strength. They will soar on wings like eagles; they will run and not grow weary, they will walk and not be faint."

After my injection on August 28th, I was forced to wait for the start of radiation treatments until November 20th. For my type A personality, this was torture.

Again, I'm the type of person who wants to solve a problem before anyone knows a problem exists. Waiting is not in my DNA.

When I lost my son in 1998 my spirit was crushed. I had to learn to wait on the Lord to allow me to walk, renew my strength and eventually help me run and soar. The verse above is easily read, but the learning experience to realize that it is true and that I can rely on God to provide it to me was painful beyond words. Once again, I was learning that He was beside me every day, and would provide for my every need.

Waiting to begin radiation was certainly easier than surviving the loss of my child, but it made me anxious because I didn't think any progress in the fight was occurring. The doctor calmed me slightly when he told me that the delay was in order to allow the hormone treatment to work and prepare cells so that the radiation treatment would be more effective.

It reminded me of the Phoney War period in World War II that occurred after Britain and France declared war on Germany on September 3, 1939 and lasted until May 10, 1940 when Germany attacked France and the Low countries.

While there wasn't a war going on in the common definition of the word, there were activities in preparation for a terrible war that would break out soon. I try to imagine what soldiers, sailors and airmen on both sides were thinking during that period. How could the public imagine that after this false peace ended on May 10th, 1940, all-out war would occur for five more years?

One of the toughest decisions that I faced was when to tell my daughter, Elizabeth. She was typically anxious leaving home for college and gaining a roommate for the first time. In addition, she went to school on a softball scholarship and had the pressure of succeeding in a twenty-plus game fall season that was a prelude to their regular spring season. I did not want to add to her load; there wasn't anything she could do for me other than pray. Because of these considerations, I decided to inform her after her fall season completed in late October.

Her fall season ended on October 21st and I didn't say anything to her during my visit after the game. The following Monday, I called her and disclosed my condition. She immediately began crying, which reinforced my decision to delay telling her until her season was completed. I told her to focus on her school work and that prayer for me was the only thing that she could do presently.

On our second call later that day, she was just short of frantic. She believed that I had a very quick and deadly cancer. Again, I comforted her that my prognosis was good, but there was a fight involved to beat the disease. I knew that when she saw me looking normal and doing my daily activities during her Thanksgiving break that she would be able to relax a little bit.

Likewise, I had to visit the oncologist's office to prepare to begin treatments. Most of the preparations were simple, but there was one that stole one of the few remaining pieces of my dignity. To prepare targets for the radiation, I was given three miniature tattoos. One was on each hip and one was below my belly button. I didn't envy the nurse who had to administer those tattoos, but I did joke with her and asked if I could request what the image would be. I'm sure she was tired of guys asking her that question, but she humored me and politely said, "No."

I felt restless because I wasn't in control and couldn't see any progress. Although things were peaceful on the outside, I was teaming with energy to fight the war against cancer because until it was fought, it couldn't be beat.

Finally, it was time for my first radiation treatment.

I Want Mine with the
Secret Sauce – 45 Times

Romans 12:12 – "Be joyful in hope, patient in affliction, faithful in prayer."

Facing forty-five treatments over a nine-week period was daunting enough. Traveling from my comfortable suburban home into Austin every morning and back seemed an even bigger challenge, as it was about thirty minutes each way during moderate traffic. In August, I was given the choice of 7:30 a.m. each weekday morning or 6:00 p.m. in the evening. Wanting to get it over with each day and fight less traffic, I chose the a.m. time.

On November 20, 2017, it began. I arrived at the facility and a technician walked into the reception area and escorted me into the areas of the building that I would get to know too well. She showed me a bank of plastic baskets where each patient had a pair of hospital pants to use. There was close to sixty baskets and each one represented a man like me who was facing this same fight. Then she showed me the changing area.

Next, she showed me what would become my favorite area. It was a small waiting area that was just for the guys waiting for treatment. Friends of mine receiving treatment at other facilities didn't have this room, and their experience was less personal than mine.

When I entered the waiting area that first day, there were three men in the room. Immediately one of them asked me what number treatment that I was on. When I said that today was my first treatment, they started telling me what treatment they were on. I was encouraged to see that they appeared normal. I inquired, "What lessons have you learned that might benefit me?" My experience to this point revealed information after the fact that would have changed some of my decisions, and I wanted to minimize that possibility as much as possible during the radiation treatment period.

A guy who was almost through with his forty-five treatments gave me the benefit of his experience. It was most helpful to me.

When it was my turn for the first treatment, the technician came back and led me toward the treatment room. I had no idea what to expect. She asked me my birthday to verify that I would receive my prescribed treatment and not someone else's.

I entered the room and an extremely large machine came into view. The technician instructed me to lie down on the table. She asked me to slide down my shorts so that the tattoos I previously received would help line up the machine. If I had to lower my shorts any further, I would have been thrown into jail. Needless to say, I felt uncomfortable each treatment.

I didn't know how the machine operated, but would learn quickly. For all of the preparation and travel involved, the treatment itself was the simplest part of the entire process. I focused on the music that was playing and after about two and a half songs, the first treatment was completed.

After the first day, I was on my own to come into the guy's waiting room and be prepared when they called my name. In that room, we were all equal. In spite of being different colors, creeds and ages, all other distinctions were not apparent. Wealth, reputation in the community, and life experiences did not matter.

We were all fighting our case of prostate cancer. Our treatments were similar only in the radiation area. Each of our other treatments varied based on our individual plans.

For the first several days, I was the rookie. Soon after, four guys that arrived just after me would share the waiting room every day.

Their fellowship made going through the treatments much easier. We would discuss everything except religion and politics. We discussed how we had arrived at this point and the treatments that we had experienced.

Those four great guys that I became closest to made the experience more enjoyable. I hope that I made the time I shared with them as pleasurable as they made it for me. What was said in the waiting room by the guys stayed in the waiting room.

Early on, it seemed like completing forty-five treatments would never occur. I was supposed to finish on January 26th, but due to machine malfunctions, weather issues and coming for make-up treatments on two Saturdays, I hoped to finish January 29th. I say that date because, like other things in life, my expected "graduation" date would remain burned into my mind.

Three technicians rotated taking care of us and did a fantastic job. They were always friendly, informative and caring which made the time positive.

Because of my sense of humor, I worked to inject humor into every part of the process that I could. It didn't take long before the daily question about my birthday seemed unnecessary. As a joke, I would say that my birthday was in 1987, which obviously wasn't accurate. I especially did this when the youngest one was working. She would ask me why I stated an incorrect date, and I said if people can deem themselves to be different than they were born why couldn't I deem myself to be born on a different date than my actual birthdate? She probably thinks I'm crazy to this day.

Next, I wanted to make sure that the technicians were giving me the best treatment. Parodying commercials from a few hamburger chains, I said, **"Please give me my treatment with the secret sauce."** The hamburger stands had their own "secret sauce" to differentiate them from their competitors and increase sales. It became a daily request, and all the technicians probably got sick of hearing it.

One day when there wasn't any music in the treatment room, I asked if I could play music off of my cell phone. Then the fun really began. I would play everything from Reggae to Texas Dance Hall music.

The guys and I would joke to each other about the pressure in receiving the treatment and that the guys ahead of us shouldn't break the machine before we could be treated. When they returned to the changing room after the treatment, they'd boast about completing another treatment and not breaking the machine. Sometimes one of the guys would happily state that his body wasn't smoking after his session.

One time the machine broke mid-session when my friend with the time slot after me was being treated. It took three hours to repair and I was grateful that I didn't have to wait an extra three hours that day like the others did.

One of the guys began timing the machine and analyzing his treatments every day. We tried anything to make those forty-five treatment days more enjoyable and less stressful.

On top of the humor, I would regularly pray during the treatment that it would be effective and that I would experience minimal side effects. I believe I was more fortunate than a lot of the guys as I didn't experience many side effects.

Every Thursday was doctor day; we would visit with the radiation oncologist after our treatment. One day he was telling me that everything was going well as he looked at the image of my pelvis on the screen, I asked him if he could see any progress in reducing my tumor. "The improvement's too small to see," he exclaimed. I expected to hear that we were kicking the tumor in the backside and I was disappointed with his response. It concerned me that we were going through all of these steps, but couldn't tell if it was working or not.

Finally, I approached the halfway point; time seemed to have picked up speed.

All of the guys that I shared the waiting room with experienced similar feelings about time. We all kept count of our treatments, observed the halfway point and then began the countdown.

After a nice weekend without having to drive into Austin for a radiation treatment, I was scheduled for my normal 7:30 a.m. session on Monday before driving to my office in College Station, Texas.

The phone awoke me on Sunday night and I was informed by the tech that my treatment that day could not be administered because the machine was broken. This happened more than once and it did not help any of us to achieve our forty-five treatments as early as we would like to have reached it.

Because I was so eager to complete this phase of the fight, I selected a route that would take me close to the doctor's office. When I entered the door around 6:45 a.m., the doctor happened to be talking to the receptionist. He had a startled look as he didn't expect to see me since I'd been informed not to come in that day.

I told him that I stopped on the chance that the repair had been completed. He confirmed that there was no change, and I left for College Station.

The next day, I related the story to the guys in the waiting room to their amusement. I told them and later the doctor that I must have contracted RWS (Radiation Withdrawal Syndrome) because I hadn't had a treatment in three days. Everyone enjoyed the humor because by that time all of the guys that I interacted with were ready to get it over with.

Later, a new guy joined us in the waiting room. He asked us for our advice. When my turn came to speak, I seriously stated that, whatever he did, he should avoid catching Radiation Withdrawal Syndrome. He listened intently to me and then nervously asked me more about the condition. My friends in the room were containing their laughter when I explained the day that I came in for a treatment in spite of being told not to because the machine was down. He looked as if he had just received a letter from the IRS.

　　　　　　　　　RICHARD V. BATTLE

After a couple of minutes, I broke the tension and told him that I made the condition up as a cover for my unsuccessful trip for treatment.

He relaxed and smiled, and we all had a big laugh. I guess you had to be there to appreciate the humor, but it was another example of how each of the guys tried to make the best of what we were experiencing.

As we reached single digits, time went faster and our eagerness to complete this phase of treatment advanced even faster. Ten, nine, eight, seven, six, five, four, three the end was finally in sight.

STRIVING TO BE A GOOD
EXAMPLE TO OTHERS

Titus 2:7 – "In everything set them an *example* by doing what is good."

I am mindful that as I go through my walk that has been filled with both joy and trials, other people observe my actions. I wish I had realized it much earlier in my life.

It is impossible for any of us to be the perfect example like Christ, but we can all strive to be the best example we can for the benefit of others.

We never know when someone is looking to us for that example, which means that we should always act as if this very moment is our time to be an example for others.

When my daughter, Elizabeth, was just learning to eat popcorn, I discovered that lesson. She was eating one piece at a time like her mother. I reached into the bowl and withdrew a handful of popcorn and put several pieces into my mouth, unaware of her observation. Within a few minutes she was stuffing her face like she had seen me do previously. Her graceful training was overturned in an instant. Thankfully, her mother was able to restore her to a more ladylike habit.

When I noticed that she'd picked up that bad habit, I began paying closer attention to my actions around her and others.

If we are to be a good example, we must focus on others more than ourselves because we realize that our actions can either lift people up or bring them down.

The guys that I met during my treatments had a variety of attitudes. Some were upbeat and others had sour attitudes. I communicated positivism daily in an effort to help everyone leave the treatment center feeling better than they did when they entered it. I sincerely hope those guys recover completely, and that my positive outlook helped their attitude and made a small contribution to their healing.

It is easier to for me to live positively and communicate that through my words and deeds because God has and will take better care of me than I deserve regardless of what happens to me here on earth.

He has not nor will He ever quit on me, and I will never quit attempting to be a better person and example every day. The following illustration is one of my favorites.

I have the utmost admiration for Winston Churchill. Just after he was elevated to prime minister in May of 1940, the United Kingdom faced one of its greatest threats. France had fallen and expectations were that Germany would attack England at any time. No one gave Great Britain any chance of defeating Hitler and the Nazis.

Because of the desperate situation, some of the leaders of Parliament pleaded with Churchill to negotiate a peace treaty to avoid war. They'd rather have been servants to Germany than to have fought for their freedom.

Churchill would have none of that. He stood alone in Parliament and roused the British people and elected officials with an electrifying speech. He ended it with a rousing declaration of his position on a negotiated peace. He said that the United Kingdom would, "NEVER QUIT, NEVER QUIT, NEVER QUIT, NEVER QUIT, NEVER, NEVER, NEVER, NEVER QUIT"!

The example of his leadership and resolve galvanized the people. Leaders in Parliament knew that negotiating away their freedom for a limited peace was not an option. From that point forward it was war with Germany until victory was secured in 1945.

Churchill's example still serves us today, but I'll bet he never worried about the long term impact of his actions because of the urgency of the current crisis he faced. It is a case in point that there is no way to know how many or which people, or for how long our example might benefit others. That uncertainty makes our actions and example even more important.

THE NEW HOPE!

Romans 15:13 – "May the God of **hope** fill you with all joy and peace as you trust **in him**, so that you may overflow with **hope** by the power of the Holy Spirit."

I Hope it Worked

Graduation Day - January 29ᵗʰ, 2018

Psalm 143:1 – "Lord, hear my prayer, listen to my cry for mercy; in your faithfulness and righteousness come to my **relief**."

As I got closer to the end, there was another patient who was finishing before me that stated what all of us in the waiting room eventually thought. We had been so focused on completing forty-five treatments that we had not thought about their impact.

As that fellow completed his last treatment and prepared to leave the facility, he stated in a matter of fact tone, "I hope it worked." When the guys in the waiting room and I heard that, our focus changed from completing the treatments to what happens next.

Our daily conversations changed from how we were feeling, our side effects and current events to what lay beyond the end of our treatments. We each had different follow-up schedules which led me to wonder if my treatment plan would be more or less effective than the other guys.

Two, one and then I had to wait another weekend because of a missed day in the schedule. Finally it was January 29, 2018, my *Graduation Day*!

The guys that I had become closest to all were finishing after me. I was excited about finishing my treatments, but also knew that the days of sharing the waiting room with them were over. They all were excited for me and congratulated me as I departed for the treatment room for the last time. I know from my experience that every time another person completed their treatment that I was excited for them, but it also made me more anxious to complete my time. I believe they most likely had similar feelings.

My favorite technician was excited for me also as she prepared me for that final treatment. I joked with her one last time about my birthday and thanked her profusely for how well she and the other technicians had taken care of me. I played my own music, which furthered my enjoyment of that last episode. At last, I had completed forty-five treatments. I exited the table and said goodbye to the guys one last time.

As I headed for the building exit, my doctor and his staff clapped and gave me a goody bag that included a replica horseshoe similar to the one that I held for every treatment. This part of the fight was over, but the war wasn't won yet.

It seemed like the seventy-one days it took to complete forty-five treatments took a long time. The following seventy-one days afterward seemed to fly by. It illustrates how our perceptions influence how we think and feel.

I asked for mercy, comfort and minimal side effects during the radiation treatments and was blessed to have received them. Now, it was time to take the next steps in my walk.

So Far So Good

Isaiah 38: 16-17 – "You restored me to health and let me live. Surely it was for my benefit that I suffered such anguish. In your love you kept me from the pit of destruction; you have put all my sins behind your back."

After completing the 45th radiation treatment, I wasn't scheduled for a doctor follow-up until March 5th. The method used to see if the treatments were successful was to measure my PSA. This first blood test would establish a new baseline to watch in the future for the return of the cancer.

Although it was hopeful that my PSA would decline, articles I read said that it could go down, up or stay close to the same. That confused me because I wanted to see progress after going through what seemed to me a lengthy treatment process. It also made me wonder about the medical profession.

I had experienced fewer side effects from the radiation than a lot of other people I compared myself against. The few that I did sustain dissipated within the next month.

Going into the treatment phase, I had been told that my previous exercise schedule would make my experience better than if I didn't routinely workout. Based on the guys with whom I interacted, it seemed to be true, and I was extremely grateful that my good physical condition benefitted me.

Regardless of fatigue or other side effects, I would strongly encourage anyone who endures cancer treatments to maintain or begin or maintain as consistent an exercise regimen as possible. It will serve you well.

As before the discovery of my cancer, I felt no symptoms after radiation. No one could tell that I had the disease or had been treated by looking at me. It made me aware that there are untold others going through similar trials. We never know which of our brothers and sisters are suffering from a disease or another issue, which makes our interaction with others more important than we might otherwise believe. We have an opportunity to lift them up and reflect the grace that we have been given toward others.

February kept me busy with projects and attending Elizabeth's college softball games, which was good, as the activities prevented me from focusing on my upcoming doctor visit.

At last, it was time to visit the doctor and see if it worked. Thankfully, my PSA was undetectable! For now, it appeared that the cancer was in remission. I recognized that God had given or allowed me to go through this experience for a reason. What it was I did not know, but I hope that I can learn it so that I don't have to suffer further for this lesson.

After the doctor left, the nurse reappeared to give me my second of three hormone shots. My testosterone was down, which in theory would deprive hidden cancer cells needed food. The second shot would continue to further reduce my testosterone level. I thought the reaction to it would be like the first shot. Quickly, I would discover that was not the case.

ROUND AND ROUND
SHE GOES

WHERE SHE STOPS NOBODY KNOWS

Psalm 145:14 – "The LORD upholds all who fall and lifts up all who are bowed down."

When I was growing up, school districts in the Dallas – Ft. Worth Metroplex had "Fair Day," which was a weekday when school was closed to allow students to attend the State Fair of Texas just southeast of downtown Dallas.

It was always fun, and became more so when I was old enough to go with friends. No one had much money to spend so managing it until it was time to go home was crucial. That meant that we spent a lot of time walking around the fairgrounds seeking activities that were free.

In those days, the Midway offered the most entertainment, but could also separate you from your money quicker. As we walked back and forth, the barkers would entice us to spend our money on the games. I think back to the ones with wheels and the barker shouting when the ball was spun, "Round and round she goes and where she stops nobody knows." In some ways, parts of my life on earth feel like that.

Almost immediately after my second shot, it seemed as if I gained about fifteen pounds. I hadn't changed my diet so I couldn't figure out what was going on. When I researched side effects of the hormone treatment, weight gain of ten to fifteen pounds was listed. Great, I thought, and not in the spirit of Tony the Tiger.

And worse, it was all around my mid-section. I hadn't planned on celebrating the end of my radiation treatments by buying a new wardrobe so I would have to further modify my diet and exercise to maintain some semblance of fitness.

In addition, I started noticing more fatigue and difficulty in accomplishing my daily exercise. My motivation

RICHARD V. BATTLE

levels to exercise also dropped. I knew that if I succumbed to this feeling that I would suffer more physical issues than if I overcame the lethargy and continued my workouts. I resolved to do so and continue playing senior softball.

Additional symptoms of the hormone treatment continued, and became the worst part of the treatment plan. I shared experiences with one of my softball teammates who also had prostate cancer. We both bemoaned the effects of the hormone treatments and desired a way to discontinue them without increasing our risk of recurring cancer.

As I write this, I'm scheduled to continue the hormone treatments for another ten months. While a vapor in the big picture of time, I'm not looking forward to it.

Then there is the unknown, which is why I recalled the bark from the state fair. The wheel is spinning and no one knows if I'll remain cancer free, or require additional treatments. Where the wheel stops nobody knows.

The decrease in my quality of life from the hormone treatment can "bow me down" occasionally, which enables the Lord to show me His grace and mercy. When I focus on myself, it is easy to get down. When I focus on the Lord and/or others, it is easy to appreciate what I have been given and how I have been blessed beyond what I deserve or more than so many others who deserved blessings more than I do. As I'll discuss further, there is a great lesson here for all of us in our daily lives.

WHAT'S NEXT?

James 1-12, "Blessed is the one who perseveres under trial because, having stood the test, that person will receive the crown of life that the Lord has promised to those who love him."

Each Day on Earth is Unknown, but the Future Beyond is Known

Ephesians 2:10 – "For we are God's handiwork, created in Christ Jesus to do good works, which God prepared in advance for us to do."

As I stated earlier, I didn't plan for these events to happen, or to write about them. I was proceeding with several other book projects when sharing this story was suggested.

After that, God took over and directed me to prioritize this volume. It wasn't due to one thing, or from one person. It was a symphony of occurrences that only God could have orchestrated.

None of us know how much time we have left on this earth. That is especially true of someone who has known heart disease and cancer.

What if the cancer returns? There is no way to know, but I do know that the remainder of my life on earth will include monitoring and watching for its return.

What if a heart issue returns? Again, there is no way to know, and I will live and monitor it as I proceed on my walk here.

No one knows what my future on earth will be. So, to use an old country saying, "I will make hay while the sun shines." For anyone not familiar with the expression, it refers to the critical importance of cutting grass, baling it and putting it away during dry weather, as rain can ruin it after it is cut

I strive to live daily the same way. While I'm on this earth, what can I do to glorify God and benefit others? These are the two most important commandments that we are given in **Matthew 22:37-39** which states,

"Jesus replied: 'Love the Lord your God with all your heart and with all your soul and with all your mind. This is the first and greatest commandment. [39] And the second is like it: 'Love your neighbor as yourself.'"

As long as I am breathing, I will continue to look for and hope to learn future lessons in order to better do so. I hope learning the new lessons isn't as painful as some of the methods that have been used to teach me previously. However, the important thing is to learn what I am supposed to and grow into the person that God wants me to be before my life is over.

While I don't know what each day on earth holds for me, I am confident because of the experience in my life that God will take me to heaven when I pass from this earth. He will do this not because of any merit of mine, but because of His faithful promises and Jesus paying for my sins. My faith enables me to live without fear of what may happen here and to look forward to what will happen for eternity.

For That I Did Well Credit God, the Rest Me

2 Corinthians 4:16-18 – "Therefore we do not lose heart. Though outwardly we are wasting away, yet inwardly we are being renewed day by day. For our light and momentary troubles are achieving for us an eternal glory that far outweighs them all. So we fix our eyes not on what is seen, but on what is unseen, since what is seen is temporary, but what is unseen is eternal."

Regardless of good health in the future or more challenges, I know that God loves me more than I deserve and that He is with me for my benefit all of the time.

After I lost my son, John, in 1998, I searched extensively for evidence that he would be in heaven when I arrived. Digging deeply into the Scriptures, I found assurance that he would meet me there for eternity.

In my effort to stem my grief for John's loss, the passage above from Corinthians became one of great comfort for me. It continues to console me when this world attempts to divert my attention off of spiritual things.

That time was also one of great reflection of my life. It was reaffirmed to me that the most successful endeavors of my life all occurred because of God's provision. It was easy to see because I knew the achievements were beyond my capability. Likewise, all of my failings were instances where I was outside God's plan for me and on my own. I failed him and continue to do so, but he has never failed me.

From this I wrote my epitaph on my headstone connected to my son's that says, "For that I did well, credit God, the rest me." In the twenty years since that time, the words I chose still guide me and inspire me to pursue living up to them daily.

We are told in **James 1-12**, **"Blessed is the one who perseveres under trial because, having stood the test, that person will receive the crown of life that the Lord has promised to those who love him."**

It is my daily desire to receive the grace that God gives me, and to live a life worthy of it. I also strive to be a good example to others in the example that Jesus provided us.

Writing this story has been very humbling. It was a burden and a responsibility to convey His message via my experience in words that I hope will benefit you in your faith and walk.

More Aha's

Proverbs 24:32 – "I applied my heart to what I observed and **learned** a lesson from what I saw:"

During the travels of my unwelcome opportunity, I also received aha's of previously learned lessons. I've denoted the most important ones below.

I'm More Accepting of my lack of control

People that have known me for a long time know that I like to control the events in my life as much as possible. I'm a stickler for being on-time and checking items off of my to-do list. When circumstances violated my planning, it would upset me a lot.

When my son passed away, I was crushed and it showed me that I was totally out of control. Through the grief of losing him and the realization that the Lord was in control and doing a much better job than I could, I began to accept that our control of most anything is an illusion.

Psalm 55:22 says, **"Cast your cares on the Lord and he will sustain you; he will never let the righteous be shaken."** If we let Him, He gives us everything we need daily.

My desire to be in control was tested one time while writing this book. A friend and I were returning to the Austin, Texas area from my daughter Elizabeth's college softball game. My new truck warned me that one tire was losing air. It decreased rapidly as I pushed to reach the next town. We made it, but there wasn't anywhere that would service a tire at 7:30 that night. We began to change the tire, which we both had done previously.

Then my new truck betrayed me. The key to unlock the spare didn't work. To make a long story short, after three hours, we received the help we needed to resume our journey.

Previously, I would have been beside myself with anger. It would have taken weeks or months for me to be able to laugh about the experiences. Thankfully, this time, I was able to laugh about the experience during and immediately after it.

Through my painfully learned experiences of losing my son, I had grown in my walk, which helped me with my health issues.

We're told in **Matthew 11:28-30, "Come to me, all you who are weary and burdened, and I will give you rest. Take my yoke upon you and learn from me, for I am gentle and humble in heart, and you will find rest for your souls. For my yoke is easy and my burden is light."**

The Lord is there for us all of the time to give us rest and to teach us.

I'm More Thankful in my daily life

The distractions of the world made it easy for me to overlook God's hand at some early points in my life. Not until I personally experienced success beyond what I knew I could achieve on my own did I fully recognize that everything good I had ever done was from God.

We are instructed in **Ephesians 5:20** to **"always giving thanks to God the Father for everything, in the name of our Lord Jesus Christ."** As I have gotten older, it is easier to see God's provision in more and more and smaller and smaller things. Every day I am thankful for the mercy that I'm given and strive to do something in His service.

I'm Blessed more than I deserve

It is easy when things are going well to forget how blessed we are. My mother would tell me when I was young how fortunate I was to live in the United States, to be healthy, to earn an education, and to be free. Honestly, I didn't fully appreciate what she was telling me until I had experienced some setbacks.

I think it is in our nature to learn more from our own experience than from the lives of others. When a young child is told not to touch a hot stove because it will burn his or her hand, guess what happens next. The child touches the stove, but only once. Oh, how I wish that I would have spent more time learning from my grandparents, parents and others who could have taught me so much more if I had taken the time to listen.

Proverbs 16:20 tells us, **"Whoever gives heed to instruction prospers, and blessed is the one who trusts in the LORD."** Tomorrow isn't promised to us, and every day is a new blessing.

My Experience helps me to Endure More than I ever thought I could

When we are children everything annoys or frustrates us because we haven't gained the maturity or experience to deal with it. If we grow normally, we will be able to face growing challenges because we learn how to overcome them with His help.

Romans 15:4 – "For everything that was written in the past was written to teach us, so that through the endurance taught in the Scriptures and the encouragement they provide we might have hope."

I have survived an apartment fire that killed my neighbor—and its aftermath, I have gone broke after fighting financial ruin for two years, and I have survived the loss of my son after what seemed like an endless period of grief.

In light of the lessons and examples of Scripture, those experiences and others had built my endurance for the experiences in this volume and more. My faith and hope in our Lord give me hope every day that regardless of what obstacles I face, that He is there beside me to help me endure them. I don't know how anyone without faith faces the major challenges of this life.

I Strive to Grow Spiritually Daily

We are charged in **2 Peter 3:18**: **"But grow in the grace and knowledge of our Lord and Savior Jesus Christ. To him be glory both now and forever! Amen."** Our choice when facing tribulation is to either grow closer to God or to grow further away from Him. The more trials that I have experienced, and the more I see our Lord's hand carrying me through them, the more motivated I am to grow closer to Him.

Since 1998 when I lost my son, one of the major teaching tools that I have enjoyed and profited from is the

Thru The Bible five-year Bible study that J. Vernon McGee began in the 1970s. I have just about completed my fourth five-year journey and I'm uplifted listening daily to the mp3 audio versions of the broadcast. In spite of what you might believe, God reveals new things to me each time I return to a section previously studied. I often listen while I'm exercising and always feel better afterward.

I Look for Opportunities Daily to Encourage Others

God loved me before I was even born and continues to provide for me and encourage me that regardless of what happens in this life, He has a place for me with Him in eternity. This is stated and promised to believers in **2 Thessalonians 2:2 – "May our Lord Jesus Christ himself and God our Father, who loved us and by his grace gave us eternal encouragement and good hope, encourage your hearts and strengthen you in every good deed and word."** That knowledge blesses my daily life.

This world can bring a person down and crush them without any feeling of remorse. It is important for me to encourage others daily. Sometimes, it is someone I know and other times it is someone whom I will never know, but with whom I will have crossed paths for a moment.

We are instructed in **1 Thessalonians 5:11, "Therefore encourage one another and build each other up, just as in fact you are doing.**" I have had people come up to me to thank me for something I shared with them years before. Most times, I don't remember the incident that they refer to. It humbles me to hear them reveal how my little bit of encouragement delivered disproportionally gigantic impacts on their lives. What a joy it is to know that you have been a small instrument to help someone's life.

Scriptures (NIV)

These Scriptures comfort me in my walk and I hope that you find solace in them also, but in no way are they the only ones that are written to lift and soothe our lives.

Exodus 14:15-16 – "Then the Lord said to Moses, 'Why are you crying out to me? Tell the Israelites to move on. Raise your staff and stretch out your hand over the sea to divide the water so that the Israelites can go through the sea on dry ground.'"

Exodus 23:20 - "See, I am sending an angel ahead of you to guard you along the way and to bring you to the place I have prepared."

Psalm 4:1 – "Answer me when I call to you, my righteous God. Give me relief from my distress; have mercy on me and hear my prayer."

Psalm 18: 2 – "The Lord is my rock, my fortress and my deliverer; my God is my rock, in whom I take refuge, my shield and the horn of my salvation, my stronghold."

Psalm 19:1 – "The heavens declare the glory of God; the skies proclaim the work of his hands."

Psalm 23:4 –"Even though I walk through the **darkest valley**, I will fear no evil, for you are with me; your rod and your staff, they comfort me."

Psalm 28:6 – "**Praise** be to **the Lord**, for he has heard my cry for mercy."

Psalm 43:3 – "Send me your light and your faithful care, let them lead me; let them bring me to your holy mountain, to the place where you dwell."

Psalm 51:10-12 – "Create in me a pure heart, O God, and renew a steadfast spirit within me. Do not cast me from your presence or take your Holy Spirit from me. Restore to me the joy of your salvation and grant me a willing spirit, to sustain me."

Psalm 55:22 – **"Cast your** cares on the Lord and he will sustain you; he will never let the righteous be shaken."

Psalm 66:20 – "Praise be to God, who has not rejected my prayer or withheld his love from me!"

Psalm 94:17-19 – "Unless the Lord had given me help, I would soon have dwelt in the silence of death. When I said, 'My foot is slipping,' your unfailing love, Lord, supported me. When anxiety was great within me, your consolation brought me joy."

Psalm 100:4 – "Enter his gates with **thanksgiving** and his courts with praise; give thanks to him and praise his name."

Psalm 143:1 – "Lord, hear my prayer, listen to my cry for mercy; in your faithfulness and righteousness come to my **relief**."

Psalm 145:14 – "The Lord upholds all who fall and lifts up all who are bowed down."

Proverbs 3:5 – "Trust in the Lord with all *your* heart and *lean not on your* own understanding;"

Proverbs 16:20 – "Whoever gives heed to instruction prospers, and blessed is the one who trusts in the Lord."

Proverbs 20:24 – "A person's steps are directed by the LORD. How then can anyone understand their own way?"

Proverbs 24:32 – "I applied my heart to what I observed and **learn**ed a lesson from what I saw:"

Isaiah 38: 16-17 – "You restored me to health and let me live. Surely it was for my benefit that I suffered such anguish. In your love you kept me from the pit of destruction; you have put all my sins behind your back."

Isaiah 40:31 – "but those who hope in the LORD will renew their strength. They will soar on wings like eagles; they will run and not grow weary, they will walk and not be faint."

Isaiah 41:10 – "So do not fear, for I am with you; do not be dismayed, for I am your God. I will strengthen you and help you; I will uphold you with my righteous right hand."

Jeremiah 29:11 – "For I know the plans I have for you," declares the Lord, "plans to prosper you and not to harm you, plans to give you hope and a future."

Matthew 8:24-26 – "Suddenly a furious storm came up on the lake, so that the waves swept over the boat. But Jesus was sleeping. The disciples went and woke him, saying, 'Lord, save us! We're going to drown!' He replied, "You of little faith, why are you so afraid?" Then he got up and rebuked the winds and the waves, and it was completely calm."

Matthew 11:28-30 - "Come to me, all you who are weary and burdened, and I will give you rest. Take my **yoke** upon you and learn from me, for I am gentle and humble in heart, and you will find rest for your souls. For my **yoke** is easy and my burden is light."

Matthew 19:26 – "Jesus looked at them and said, '*With* man this is impossible, but *with God all things are possible.*'"

Matthew 22:37-39 – "Jesus replied: 'Love the Lord your God with all your heart and with all your soul and with all your mind. This is the first and greatest commandment. [39] And the second is like it: 'Love your neighbor as yourself.'"

John 8:12 – "When Jesus spoke again to the people, he said, 'I am the **light** of the world. Whoever follows me will never walk in darkness, but will have the **light** of life.'"

John 16-33 - "I have told you these things, so *that* in me you may have *peace*. In this world you will have trouble. But take heart! I have overcome the world."

Romans 5:2-5 – "…through whom we have gained access by faith into this grace in which we now stand.

And we boast in the hope of the glory of God. Not only so, but we also glory in our sufferings, because we know that suffering produces perseverance, perseverance character; and character, hope. And hope does not put us to shame, because God's love has been poured out into our hearts through the Holy Spirit, who has been given to us."

Romans 8:28 – "And we know that in all *things* God works for the *good* of those who love him, who have been called according *to* his purpose."

Romans 12:12 – "Be joyful in hope, patient in affliction, faithful in prayer."

Romans 15:4 – "For everything that was written in the past was written to teach us, so that through the endurance taught in the Scriptures and the encouragement they provide we might have hope."

Romans 15:13 – "May the God of **hope** fill you with all joy and peace as you trust **in him**, so that you may overflow with **hope** by the power of the Holy Spirit."

Ephesians 2:10 – "For we are God's handiwork, created in Christ Jesus to do good works, which God prepared in advance for us to do."

Ephesians 5:20 – "Always giving thanks to God the Father for everything, in the name of our Lord Jesus Christ.

Philippians 4: 6-7 – "Do not be anxious about anything, but in every situation, by prayer and petition, with thanksgiving, present your requests to God. And the peace of God, which transcends all understanding, will guard your hearts and your minds in Christ Jesus."

1 Corinthians 2:9-10 – "However, as it is written: 'What no eye has seen, what no ear has heard, and what no human mind has conceived'— the things God has prepared for those who love him—these are the things God has revealed to us by his Spirit."

2 Corinthians 1:3-5 – "Praise be to the God and Father of our Lord Jesus Christ, the Father of compassion and the God of all comfort, who comforts us in all our troubles, so that we can comfort those in any trouble with the comfort we ourselves have received from God. For just as the sufferings of Christ flow over into our lives, so also through Christ our comfort overflows."

2 Corinthians 4:16-18 – "Therefore we do not lose heart. Though outwardly we are wasting away, yet inwardly we are being renewed day by day. For our light and momentary troubles are achieving for us an eternal glory that far outweighs them all. So we fix our eyes not on what is seen, but on what is unseen, since what is seen is temporary, but what is unseen is eternal."

2 Corinthians 12:9 – "But he said to me, 'My grace is sufficient for you, for my power is made perfect in weakness.' Therefore I will boast all the more gladly about my weaknesses, so that Christ's power may rest on me."

1 Thessalonians 5:11 – "Therefore **encourage** one another and build each other up, just as in fact you are doing."

2 Thessalonians 2:2 – "May our Lord Jesus Christ himself and God our Father, who loved us and by his grace gave us eternal encouragement and good hope, encourage your hearts and strengthen you in every good deed and word."

Titus 2:7 – "In everything set them an *example* by doing what is good."

Hebrews 11:1 – "Now faith is confidence in what we hope for and assurance about what we do not see."

James 1-12 – "Blessed is the one who perseveres under trial because, having stood the test, that person will receive the crown of life that the Lord has promised to those who love him."

2 Peter 3:18 – "But grow in the grace and knowledge of our Lord and Savior Jesus Christ. To him be glory both now and forever! Amen."

Quotes

"The secret to success in life is not how many times you get knocked down in life, but how many times you get back up." – T. Bubba Bechtol

"Never quit, never quit, never quit, never quit, never quit, never, never, never quit." – Winston Churchill

"When the storm clouds come, the eagle flies and the small birds run for cover." – Lewis Timberlake

"Time is your enemy disguised as your friend." – Dr. Haddon Robinson

"Be sure you're right and go ahead" – Davy Crockett

"Challenges that are bigger than men, make men bigger." - Anonymous

"A man's mind once expanded by a new idea can never return to its previous state." – Oliver Wendell Holmes

COVER PHOTO STORY

Psalm 23:4 – "Even though I walk through the **darkest valley**, I will fear no evil, for you are with me; your rod and your staff, they comfort me."

John 8:12 – "When Jesus spoke again to the people, he said, 'I am the **light** of the world. Whoever follows me will never walk in darkness, but will have the **light** of life.'"

I had already given thought to the image that I wanted on the cover of this book. Previously, I had chosen photos from commercial sources and prepared to do so again.

A solid forbidding wall of dark clouds represents us when facing life's challenges alone. The radiant light of God shining through that dark wall of clouds provides us grace and hope in our hour of need.

On April 14, 2018 as I was driving to my softball tournament, I looked to my left and was awestruck. The perfect image I desired was painted in the sky in front of me. I couldn't believe my good fortune and was humbled to believe God put it there to encourage me and for me to use in this volume.

BACK COVER PHOTO STORY

Psalm 19:1 – "The heavens declare the glory of God; the skies proclaim the work of his hands."

After identifying the perfect picture that showed the dark clouds that I was under and God's light shining thru to encourage me, I wanted to add an image on the back cover that would illustrate the results of passing through the dark valley.

I was at Elizabeth's last home college softball game on April 26, 2018, when I saw the image. Sitting in the stands that were bathed in bright sunshine, a single, solitary cirrus cloud appeared beyond the field. It slowly floated from left to right and appeared to me as God's handiwork.

It's as if this cloud fit the hole that allowed God's light to shine through the wall of clouds on the cover picture.

To me, this cloud declares His glory and total control over this universe and everything in it. Relying on His promises, I can live on earth comforted by Him regardless of what I experience.

BIBLIOGRAPHY

Garrison, Webb. *Why You Say It*. Nashville: Thomas Nelson, 1992.

Life Application Study Bible- NIV. Carol Stream, Illinois and Grand Rapids, Michigan: Tyndale House and Zondervan, 1997

McGee, J. Vernon. *Thru The Bible*. Nashville: Thomas Nelson 1982 (six volume printed version) Audio version available on radio, cd and flash drive

www.Biblegateway.com   -Versions
                         - NIV
                         - Living Bible

ABOUT THE AUTHOR

Richard Battle previously authored *Surviving Grief by God's Grace* and was an adult Sunday school teacher for twenty two years.

Richard has also authored *The Four Letter Word That Builds Character*, *The Master's Sales Secrets*, and *The Volunteer Handbook – How to Organize and Manage a Successful Organization*. He has served on the board of many organizations including Alpha Kappa Psi, The John Ben Shepperd Public Leadership Foundation, Boy Scouts of America, Muscular Dystrophy Association and Keep Austin Beautiful.

He has been a public speaker and trainer for over 30 years on topics including; volunteerism, leadership, sales and faith.

He was appointed by Texas Governor Rick Perry to The Texas Judicial Council and The Texas Emerging Technology Fund.

As president of the Austin Junior Chamber of Commerce (1983-1984), the U.S. Junior Chamber of Commerce recognized the chapter as the Most Outstanding chapter in the United States, and the Junior Chamber of Commerce International recognized Richard as the Outstanding Chapter President in the world.

Richard was an executive with KeyTrak (a Reynolds and Reynolds company), and has more than 40 years of experience in sales, executive management and leadership. He was selected to the National Register's Who's Who in Executives and Professionals in 2005.

Richard lives in Texas

CPSIA information can be obtained
at www.ICGtesting.com
Printed in the USA
LVHW09s2140181018
594096LV00001B/11/P